Gluten-Free

BREADS

What is Gluten?

Gluten is a protein that is found in wheat, rye, and barley. There are many reasons people avoid gluten. Some people are allergic to wheat itself while others may have a sensitivity to gluten and just feel better when they avoid it. The most serious is Celiac Disease, in which the body produces an autoimmune response after eating gluten. The only way to manage this condition is to follow a strict gluten-free diet.

No More Bread? No Pasta?

At first, going gluten-free may appear to be rather limiting. Fortunately, there are many more delicious foods on the gluten-free list than on the forbidden list. There are also more and more products, from cereals to baking mixes to pastas, which are now being formulated in gluten-free versions. These days you'll find them not just in health food stores and online, but also on the shelves of most major supermarkets.

Some Good News

Spotting hidden gluten in processed foods is a lot easier now thanks to the FDA's Food Allergy Labeling Law that went into effect in 2004. Since wheat is a common allergen, any product that contains wheat or is derived from it must say so on the label. That means formerly questionable ingredients, such as modified food starch or maltodextrin, must now show wheat as part of their name if they were made from it (for example, "wheat maltodextrin"). Be aware that this ONLY applies to foods produced in the US and Canada. Imports are a different matter.

More Good News

Look at your dietary restrictions as an opportunity to try new foods. Add quinoa and chickpea flour to your cupboard. Use corn tortillas to make sandwiches or lasagna. You'll find easy recipes in this book that are so delicious you'll forget that they're gluten-free. Healthy eating may actually be easier without gluten, too. Adding more fresh produce to your meals, eating less processed food and avoiding refined flour are all steps to a better diet for anyone.

Gluten-Free Flour Blends

While there are many products that are now readily available in the supermarkets, they can be rather expensive. We have provided two basic flour blends that can be prepared in bulk and kept on hand for use at any time. Please refer to these when preparing many of the recipes in this book.

Gluten-Free All-Purpose Flour Blend

- **1 cup white rice flour**
- **1 cup sorghum flour**
- **1 cup tapioca flour**
- **1 cup cornstarch**
- **1 cup almond flour or coconut flour**

Combine all ingredients in large bowl. Whisk to make sure flours are evenly distributed. The recipe can be doubled or tripled. Store in airtight container in the refrigerator.

Makes about 5 cups

Gluten-Free Flour Blend for Breads

- **1 cup brown rice flour**
- **1 cup sorghum flour**
- **1 cup tapioca flour**
- **1 cup cornstarch**
- **³/₄ cup millet flour***
- **¹/₃ cup instant mashed potato flakes**

If millet flour is not available substitute chickpea flour.

Combine all ingredients in large bowl. Whisk to make sure ingredients are evenly distributed. The recipe can be doubled or tripled. Store in airtight container in refrigerator.

Makes about 5 cups

Orange-Lemon Citrus Bread

1³/₄ cups Gluten-Free
   All-Purpose Flour Blend
   (page 5),* plus additional
   for pan

³/₄ cup sugar

1 tablespoon plus
   ¹/₂ teaspoon grated lemon
   peel, divided

2 teaspoons baking powder

1 teaspoon xanthan gum

¹/₄ teaspoon salt

1 cup milk

¹/₂ cup vegetable oil

1 egg, beaten

1 teaspoon vanilla

¹/₄ cup orange marmalade

*Or use any all-purpose gluten-free flour
blend that does not contain xanthan gum.

1. Preheat oven to 350°F. Grease 9X5-inch loaf pan; dust with flour blend.

2. Combine 1³/₄ cups flour blend, sugar, 1 tablespoon lemon peel, baking powder, xanthan gum and salt in large bowl; mix well. Whisk milk, oil, egg and vanilla in small bowl until well blended.

3. Make well in flour mixture; pour in milk mixture and stir just until blended. (Batter will be thin.) Pour into prepared pan.

4. Bake 45 minutes or until toothpick inserted into center comes out clean. Cool in pan on wire rack 5 minutes.

5. Meanwhile, combine marmalade and remaining ¹/₂ teaspoon lemon peel in small microwavable bowl. Microwave on HIGH 15 seconds or until slightly melted.

6. Remove bread to wire rack. Spread marmalade mixture evenly over top. Cool completely before serving.

Makes 1 loaf
(about 12 servings)

Cinnamon Raisin Bread

3 cups Gluten-Free Flour Blend for Breads (page 5), plus additional for pan and work surface

$^1/_3$ cup sugar

1 tablespoon ground cinnamon

2 packages ($^1/_4$ ounce each) active dry yeast

2 teaspoons xanthan gum

1 teaspoon salt

$1^1/_4$ cups plus 2 tablespoons warm milk, divided

$^1/_4$ cup vegetable oil

2 eggs

1 tablespoon honey or maple syrup

1 teaspoon cider vinegar

$^3/_4$ cup raisins

1 tablespoon gluten-free oats (optional)

1. Line 9X5-inch loaf pan* with foil, extending sides of foil 3 inches from top of pan. Spray with nonstick cooking spray; dust with flour blend.

2. Combine sugar and cinnamon in small bowl; mix well. Set aside.

3. Combine 3 cups flour blend, yeast, xanthan gum and salt in large bowl; mix well. Whisk $1^1/_4$ cups warm milk, oil, eggs, honey and vinegar in medium bowl until well blended. Beat into flour mixture with electric mixer at low speed until batter is smooth, shiny and thick. Beat at medium-high speed 5 minutes, scraping bowl occasionally. Stir in raisins.

4. Place large sheet of parchment paper on work surface; sprinkle with flour blend. Scoop batter onto center of paper. Using dampened hands or oiled spatula, spread batter into 9X18-inch rectangle. Brush with remaining 2 tablespoons warm milk. Sprinkle evenly with all but 1 tablespoon cinnamon-sugar mixture, leaving 1-inch border.

5. Using parchment paper, roll dough jelly-roll style, beginning at short end. Push ends in to fit length of pan; trim excess paper. Using parchment paper, lift roll and place in prepared pan. (Leave parchment paper in pan.) Sprinkle with remaining 1 tablespoon cinnamon-sugar and oats, if desired.

6. Cover with lightly oiled plastic wrap; let rise in warm place 20 to 30 minutes or until batter reaches top of pan.

7. Preheat oven to 375°F. Bake 35 to 45 minutes or until bread sounds hollow when tapped and internal temperature is 200°F. Remove bread from pan; remove parchment paper and foil. Cool completely on wire rack.

Makes 1 loaf (about 12 servings)

*Do not use a glass loaf pan.

Chocolate Chip Scones

2 cups Gluten-Free All-Purpose Flour Blend (page 5),* plus additional for work surface

1/4 cup sugar

2 1/2 teaspoons baking powder

3/4 teaspoon salt

3/4 teaspoon xanthan gum

1/2 teaspoon baking soda

1/2 cup (1 stick) cold butter, cut into small pieces

1 cup semisweet chocolate chips, divided

1/2 cup plain yogurt

3/4 cup milk

*Or use any all-purpose gluten-free flour blend that does not contain xanthan gum.

1. Preheat oven to 425°F.

2. Combine 2 cups flour blend, sugar, baking powder, salt, xanthan gum and baking soda in large bowl; mix well. Cut in butter with pastry blender or two knives until coarse crumbs form. Stir in 1/2 cup chocolate chips.

3. Place yogurt in small bowl; stir in milk until well blended. Gradually add to flour mixture; stir just until dough begins to form. (You may not need all of yogurt mixture.)

4. Transfer dough to floured surface. Knead five or six times or until dough forms. Divide into three pieces. Pat each piece into circle about 1/2 inch thick. Cut each circle into six wedges using floured knife. Place 2 inches apart on ungreased baking sheets.

5. Bake 10 to 14 minutes or until lightly browned. Cool on wire rack.

6. Meanwhile, place remaining 1/2 cup chocolate chips in small resealable food storage bag; seal bag. Microwave on HIGH at 30-second intervals until chocolate is melted. Knead bag until smooth. Cut off tiny corner of bag; drizzle chocolate over scones. Let stand until set.

Makes 18 scones

Date & Walnut Bread

$^3/_4$ **cup chopped pitted dates (8 to 10 Medjool dates)**

1 **cup boiling water**

$^1/_2$ **cup brown rice flour**

$^1/_2$ **cup almond flour**

$^1/_2$ **cup cornstarch**

$^1/_4$ **cup tapioca flour**

$^1/_4$ **cup gluten-free oat flour**

1 **tablespoon baking powder**

1 **teaspoon xanthan gum**

1 **teaspoon baking soda**

$^1/_2$ **teaspoon salt**

$^1/_2$ **teaspoon ground cardamom**

1 **cup packed brown sugar**

$^1/_4$ **cup canola oil**

2 **eggs**

1 **teaspoon vanilla**

1 **cup walnuts, coarsely chopped**

1. Preheat oven to 350°F. Grease 9X5-inch loaf pan. Soak dates in boiling water in small bowl until dates are softened; cool slightly.

2. Combine brown rice flour, almond flour, cornstarch, tapioca flour, oat flour, baking powder, xanthan gum, baking soda, salt and cardamom in medium bowl.

3. Whisk brown sugar and oil in large bowl. Add eggs, one at a time, whisking well after each addition. Gradually stir in dates with water and vanilla. Beat into flour mixture just until combined. Fold in walnuts. Pour into prepared pan.

4. Bake 50 to 55 minutes or until toothpick inserted into center comes out clean. (Check after 35 minutes and cover with foil to prevent overbrowning, if necessary.) Cool in pan 10 minutes. Remove to wire rack; cool completely.

Makes 1 loaf
(about 12 servings)

Multigrain Sandwich Bread

1 cup brown rice flour, plus additional for pan

1³/₄ cups warm water (110°F)

2 tablespoons honey

1 tablespoon active dry yeast (about 1¹/₂ packages)

³/₄ cup white rice flour

²/₃ cup dry milk powder

¹/₂ cup gluten-free oat flour

¹/₃ cup cornstarch

¹/₃ cup potato starch

¹/₄ cup teff flour

2 teaspoons xanthan gum

2 teaspoons egg white powder

1¹/₂ teaspoons salt

1 teaspoon unflavored gelatin

2 eggs

¹/₄ cup canola oil

1. Preheat oven to 350°F. Grease 10X5-inch loaf pan; dust with brown rice flour.

2. Combine warm water, honey and yeast in medium bowl. Cover with plastic wrap; let stand 10 minutes or until foamy.

3. Combine 1 cup brown rice flour, white rice flour, milk powder, oat flour, cornstarch, potato starch, teff flour, xanthan gum, egg white powder, salt and gelatin in large bowl. Stir until well blended.

4. Whisk eggs and oil in small bowl. Gradually beat yeast mixture and egg mixture into flour mixture with electric mixer at low speed until combined. Beat at high speed 5 minutes or until smooth. Pour into prepared pan.

5. Bake 1 hour or until internal temperature reaches 200°F. Remove to wire rack; cool completely.

Makes 1 loaf
(about 12 servings)

Zucchini Bread

2$\frac{1}{2}$ cups Gluten-Free
  All-Purpose Flour Blend
  (page 5)*

$\frac{2}{3}$ cup packed brown sugar

$\frac{1}{2}$ cup teff flour

$\frac{1}{3}$ cup granulated sugar

1 tablespoon baking powder

2 teaspoons ground
  cinnamon

1 teaspoon baking soda

1 teaspoon salt

$\frac{3}{4}$ teaspoon xanthan gum

$\frac{1}{4}$ teaspoon ground allspice

$\frac{1}{4}$ teaspoon ground nutmeg

$\frac{1}{4}$ teaspoon ground
  cardamom

1$\frac{1}{4}$ cups whole milk

2 eggs

$\frac{1}{4}$ cup canola oil

1 teaspoon vanilla

1$\frac{1}{2}$ cups grated zucchini,
  squeezed dry

*Or use any all-purpose gluten-free flour
blend that does not contain xanthan gum.

1. Preheat oven to 350°F. Grease 9X5-inch loaf pan.

2. Combine flour blend, brown sugar, teff flour, granulated sugar, baking powder, cinnamon, baking soda, salt, xanthan gum, allspice, nutmeg and cardamom in large bowl; mix well. Whisk milk, eggs, oil and vanilla in medium bowl until well blended.

3. Make well in flour mixture; pour in milk mixture and stir just until blended. Stir in zucchini. Pour into prepared pan.

4. Bake 1 hour or until toothpick inserted into center comes out almost clean. Cool in pan on wire rack 5 minutes. Remove to wire rack; cool completely.

*Makes 1 loaf
(about 12 servings)*

Breadsticks

3½ cups Gluten-Free Flour Blend for Breads (page 5)

1 package (¼ ounce) active dry yeast

2 teaspoons salt

1½ teaspoons xanthan gum

1 teaspoon unflavored gelatin

1⅓ cups warm water (110°F)

4 tablespoons olive oil, divided

1 tablespoon honey

2 to 4 cloves garlic, minced

1. Combine flour blend, yeast, salt, xanthan gum and gelatin in food processor; process until combined. With motor running, add warm water, 2 tablespoons oil and honey. Process 30 seconds or until thoroughly combined. (Dough will be sticky.) Transfer to large greased bowl.

2. Shape dough into ball with damp hands. Cover; let rise in warm place 45 minutes. Punch down dough; let rest 15 minutes.

3. Preheat oven to 450°F. Line baking sheets with parchment paper.

4. Roll 1½-inch portions of dough into 8-inch-long ropes on clean work surface. Transfer to prepared baking sheets.

5. Bake 10 minutes. Meanwhile, combine remaining 2 tablespoons oil and garlic in small bowl; mix well. Remove breadsticks from oven; brush with garlic mixture. Bake 10 minutes or until browned. Remove to wire racks to cool slightly. Serve warm.

Makes 15 to 20 breadsticks

Variation: For a sesame seed or poppy seed topping, brush breadsticks lightly with water and sprinkle evenly with seeds before baking.

Tip: Be sure to rotate pans once during baking so that the breadsticks brown evenly.

Loaded Banana Bread

$1/2$ cup (1 stick) butter, softened

$1/2$ cup granulated sugar

$1/2$ cup packed light brown sugar

$1/4$ cup sour cream

$1 1/2$ teaspoons baking powder

$1/2$ teaspoon baking soda

$1 1/2$ cups mashed bananas (about 3 ripe bananas)

$1/2$ teaspoon vanilla

2 eggs

$1 1/2$ cups Gluten-Free All-Purpose Flour Blend (page 5)*

1 teaspoon xanthan gum

$1/4$ teaspoon salt

1 can (8 ounces) crushed pineapple, drained

$1/3$ cup flaked coconut

$1/4$ cup mini semisweet chocolate chips

*Or use any all-purpose gluten-free flour blend that does not contain xanthan gum.

1. Preheat oven to 350°F. Spray 9X5-inch loaf pan with nonstick cooking spray.

2. Beat butter, granulated sugar and brown sugar in large bowl with electric mixer at medium speed until light and fluffy. Stir sour cream, baking powder and baking soda in small bowl until dissolved. Add sour cream mixture, bananas and vanilla to butter mixture; beat just until combined. Beat in eggs, one at a time, scraping down sides of bowl after each addition.

3. Combine flour blend, xanthan gum and salt in small bowl; mix well. Gradually add flour mixture to butter mixture, beating just until combined. Fold in pineapple, coconut and chocolate chips. Pour into prepared pan.

4. Bake 1 hour and 15 minutes or until toothpick inserted into center comes out almost clean. Cool in pan on wire rack 1 hour. Remove to wire rack; cool completely.

Makes 1 loaf (about 12 servings)

Apricot-Cranberry Holiday Bread

2 cups Gluten-Free All-Purpose Flour Blend (page 5),* plus additional for pan

$1/2$ cup dried apricots, chopped

$1/2$ cup dried cranberries, chopped

3 tablespoons orange juice

$2/3$ cup plus $1/4$ cup warm water (110°F), divided

1 package ($1/4$ ounce) active dry yeast

3 tablespoons sugar, divided

$1^1/2$ teaspoons xanthan gum

$1/2$ teaspoon salt

$1/2$ teaspoon ground ginger

$1/2$ teaspoon ground nutmeg

5 tablespoons butter, melted and cooled slightly

3 eggs, at room temperature

$1/2$ cup chopped toasted pecans**

*Or use any all-purpose gluten-free flour blend that does not contain xanthan gum.

**To toast pecans, spread in a single layer on ungreased baking sheet. Bake in preheated 350°F oven 8 to 10 minutes or until fragrant, stirring occasionally.

1. Spray 9-inch square baking pan with nonstick cooking spray; dust with flour blend.

2. Combine apricots, cranberries and orange juice in small microwavable bowl. Cover and microwave on HIGH 25 to 35 seconds to soften; set aside. Combine $1/4$ cup warm water, yeast and 1 tablespoon sugar in large bowl; let stand 10 minutes or until foamy.

3. Add 2 cups flour blend, remaining 2 tablespoons sugar, xanthan gum, salt, ginger and nutmeg to yeast mixture. Whisk butter, eggs and remaining $2/3$ cup warm water in small bowl until well blended. Gradually beat into flour mixture with electric mixer at low speed until well blended. Scrape side of bowl; beat at medium-high speed 3 minutes or until well blended.

4. Drain apricot mixture; pat dry. Fold apricot mixture and pecans into batter. Pour into prepared pan. Cover and let rise in warm place 1 hour or until batter almost reaches top of pan.

5. Preheat oven to 350°F. Bake 35 to 40 minutes or until toothpick inserted into center comes out clean. Cool in pan on wire rack 10 minutes. Remove to wire rack; cool completely.

Makes 1 loaf (about 12 servings)

Chocolate Cherry Bread

$^2\!/_3$ **cup plus $^1\!/_4$ cup warm water (110°F), divided**

3 **tablespoons sugar, divided**

1 **package ($^1\!/_4$ ounce) active dry yeast**

2 **cups Gluten-Free All-Purpose Flour Blend (page 5)***

$1^1\!/_2$ **teaspoons xanthan gum**

$^1\!/_2$ **teaspoon salt**

5 **tablespoons butter, melted and cooled**

3 **eggs, at room temperature**

$^3\!/_4$ **cup dried sour cherries****

4 **ounces bittersweet chocolate, chopped**

Or use any all-purpose gluten-free flour blend that does not contain xanthan gum.

**If dried sour cherries aren't available, substitute other dried cherries or dried cranberries.*

1. Spray 9X5-inch loaf pan with nonstick cooking spray. Combine $^1\!/_4$ cup warm water, 1 tablespoon sugar and yeast in large bowl; let stand 10 minutes or until foamy.

2. Add flour blend, remaining 2 tablespoons sugar, xanthan gum and salt to yeast mixture. Whisk butter, eggs and remaining $^2\!/_3$ cup warm water in small bowl. Gradually beat into flour mixture with electric mixer at low speed until well blended. Scrape side of bowl; beat at medium-high speed 3 minutes or until well blended. Add cherries and chocolate; beat at low speed just until combined.

3. Pour batter into prepared pan. Cover and let rise in warm place about 1 hour or until batter almost reaches top of pan.

4. Preheat oven to 350°F. Bake 35 to 40 minutes or until toothpick inserted into center comes out clean. Cool in pan on wire rack 10 minutes. Remove to wire rack; cool completely.

Makes 1 loaf (about 12 servings)

Note: This bread may fall slightly after coming out of the oven.

Lemon Poppy Seed Muffins

2 cups Gluten-Free All-Purpose Flour Blend (page 5)*

1¼ cups granulated sugar

¼ cup poppy seeds

2 tablespoons plus 2 teaspoons grated lemon peel, divided

1 tablespoon baking powder

¾ teaspoon xanthan gum

½ teaspoon baking soda

½ teaspoon ground cardamom

¼ teaspoon salt

2 eggs

½ cup (1 stick) butter, melted

½ cup milk

½ cup plus 2 tablespoons lemon juice, divided

1 cup powdered sugar

Additional grated lemon peel (optional)

*Or use any all-purpose gluten-free flour blend that does not contain xanthan gum.

1. Preheat oven to 400°F. Grease 18 standard (2½-inch) muffin cups or line with paper baking cups.

2. Combine flour blend, granulated sugar, poppy seeds, 2 tablespoons lemon peel, baking powder, xanthan gum, baking soda, cardamom and salt in large bowl. Beat eggs in medium bowl. Add butter, milk and ½ cup lemon juice; mix well. Stir into flour mixture just until blended. Spoon batter evenly into prepared muffin cups.

3. Bake 15 to 20 minutes or until toothpick inserted into centers comes out clean. Cool in pans on wire racks 10 minutes.

4. Combine powdered sugar and remaining 2 teaspoons lemon peel in small bowl; stir in enough remaining lemon juice to make pourable glaze. Place muffins on sheet of foil or waxed paper. Spoon glaze over muffins. Garnish with additional lemon peel. Serve warm or at room temperature.

Makes 18 muffins

Cornmeal Pecan Muffins

1 cup Gluten-Free All-Purpose Flour Blend (page 5)*

1 cup cornmeal

1 cup sugar

1¹/₂ teaspoons baking powder

1 teaspoon baking soda

¹/₂ teaspoon salt

¹/₂ teaspoon xanthan gum

1 cup low-fat buttermilk

2 eggs

¹/₄ cup (¹/₂ stick) butter, melted

¹/₄ cup chopped pecans, toasted**

*Or use any all-purpose gluten-free flour blend that does not contain xanthan gum.

**To toast pecans, spread in a single layer on ungreased baking sheet. Bake in preheated 350°F oven 8 to 10 minutes or until fragrant, stirring occasionally.

1. Preheat oven to 350°F. Grease 12 standard (2¹/₂-inch) muffin cups or line with paper baking cups.

2. Combine flour blend, cornmeal, sugar, baking powder, baking soda, salt and xanthan gum in large bowl; mix well. Whisk buttermilk, eggs and butter in medium bowl until well blended. Stir buttermilk mixture into cornmeal mixture just until moistened. (Batter will be thick.) Fold in pecans. Spoon evenly into prepared muffin cups.

3. Bake 18 to 20 minutes or until lightly browned and toothpick inserted into centers comes out clean. Cool in pan 5 minutes; remove to wire rack. Serve warm or cool completely.

Makes 12 muffins

Sweet Cherry Biscuits

2 cups gluten-free biscuit baking mix, plus additional for work surface

¹/₄ cup sugar

2 teaspoons baking powder

¹/₂ teaspoon salt

¹/₂ teaspoon dried rosemary

¹/₂ cup (1 stick) unsalted butter, cut into small pieces

³/₄ cup milk

¹/₂ cup dried sweetened cherries, chopped

1. Preheat oven to 425°F.

2. Combine 2 cups baking mix, sugar, baking powder, salt and rosemary in large bowl. Cut in butter with pastry blender or two knives until coarse crumbs form. Stir in milk to form sticky dough. Fold in cherries.

3. Pat dough to 1-inch thickness on surface lightly dusted with baking mix. Cut out circles with 3-inch biscuit cutter. Place 1 inch apart on baking sheet.

4. Bake 15 minutes or until golden brown. Cool on wire rack 5 minutes; serve warm.

Makes 10 biscuits